Getting Started

Fabrics

An array of different fabrics that are commonly used for embroidery are shown in the photograph below. Your project and personal taste will determine the fabric to use for a project. We have used linen, denim, felt, muslin and cotton fabrics for the projects in this book, and have used cotton backing fabric for the wall hangings.

When preparing fabric for embroidery, be sure to cut a large enough piece for your finished project, including whatever margin is needed for finishing. Overcast or machine zigzag the raw edges to prevent raveling. If you use a stretchy fabric, you may want to add a cotton backing before embroidering so that the design does not get distorted.

Needles

Use one of several kinds of sharp-pointed needles (called embroidery, crewel, sharps, sewing, etc.) for embroidery. Tapestry needles, which have blunt points, are used when it is important to stitch between fabric threads without splitting them.

Needles are sized by number with the highest number being the smallest and thinnest needle. When deciding what size needle to use, choose one that is easy to thread with the amount of thread required, but is not so large that it will leave holes in the fabric.

Threads

We used DMC six-strand cotton floss for the embroidery projects in this book, and also provided color conversions for Anchor floss.

The companies have different color ranges, so these are only suggested color substitutions. Six-strand floss can be divided to work with one, two or more strands at a time, and we have noted in the diagrams how many strands to use for each section of embroidery.

Cut the thread into comfortable working lengths. We suggest about 18 inches. When working with several colors, it is helpful to thread several needles in advance so they are ready to go when you want to change colors.

Trims

Some of our projects have been enhanced with the use of beads, ribbons, buttons, and other trims. You can use your choice of trims to add your own touch to these projects.

Hoops & Frames

The use of a hoop or frame to hold your stitching is optional, depending on personal preference and/or choice of fabric. If you like a hoop, choose a clean plastic or wood version with a screw-type tension adjuster. Be sure to remove the hoop when you are not stitching and avoid crushing stitched areas as you progress.

Introduction

If you thought embroidery was tedious and too time-consuming, you'll be pleasantly surprised. Using just 12 embroidery stitches, which are illustrated at the start of the book, you can complete all of the beautiful easy-to-embroider designs in this book.

We have included quick and easy cards and gift boxes, stylish framed florals, lively floral towels, adorable clothing patches, and a variety of pillows and wall hangings for any room in your home.

Instructions are included for completing the projects exactly as shown, with many colorful touches such as beads, buttons, cording, ribbons and trims added to the designs. You can also enjoy adding your own favorite embellishments to personalize your project.

Contents

Beginning & Ending Threads

To begin an area of work where there is no previous stitching, you can hold an inch of the thread end against the back of the fabric and anchor it with your first few stitches.

You can also begin with one of the following versions of a waste knot. For a **Basic Waste Knot** (Fig 1) make a small knot at the end of the thread; stitch down into fabric a distance ahead of (and in the path of) your first few stitches with the knot on the surface of the fabric. Bring needle up and work a few stitches, anchoring the thread on the back. When the knot is reached, cut it off.

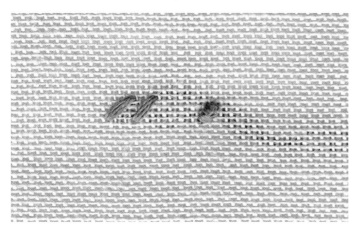

Fig 1

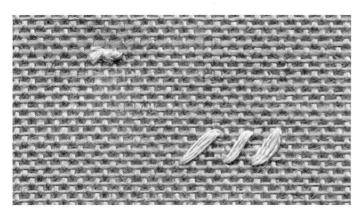

For an **Away Waste Knot** (Fig 2), make a small knot 2 or 3 inches from your beginning stitch (and away from the working area) so the knot is on the surface of the fabric. Bring needle up and work stitches. Later, cut off the waste knot, thread the beginning thread into a needle, and weave it through some completed stitches on the back of the fabric.

Fig 2

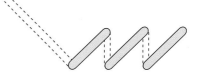

For a **Needle Waste Knot** (Fig 3), insert one end of thread into a needle and park it away from the working area; it can be secured by wrapping thread around needle once or twice to anchor. Thread opposite end of thread into another needle; stitch down then bring needle up to begin stitching. Later, undo the parked needle, bring thread to back, and weave through the beginning stitches. This is especially helpful when you want the thread to be placed in a certain direction on the back.

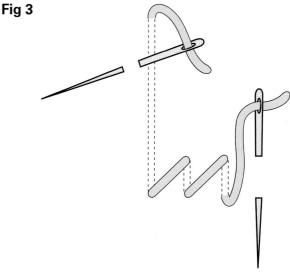

Fig 3

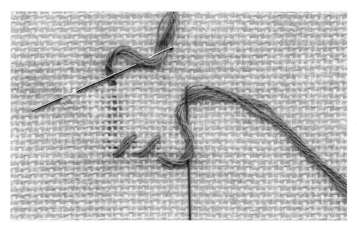

To finish threads and begin new ones next to existing stitches, weave through the backs of several stitches, preferably of the same color. Do not carry your thread any distance across the back of your work as it may show through to the front.

Transfer Techniques

There are many ways to transfer the outline of the design onto your fabric. The method you choose depends on your own preference and choice of fabric. We recommend testing the method you choose before you start.

If your fabric is sheer enough, place it directly over the design and trace it. If the fabric is heavy, using a lightbox or a sunny window will be helpful. First trace the design onto paper, then tape the fabric over the design on a light source and retrace the design onto the fabric.

Water-soluble fabric marking pens work well, but be sure to follow the manufacturer's instructions and remove pen lines before applying any heat. You can also use a #2 lead pencil for light to medium colored fabrics or a white or silver fabric-marking pencil for darker fabrics.

For heavier fabrics, you can also use an iron-on transfer pen. Trace design onto smooth paper such as typing paper with transfer pen; place ink side down on fabric. Hold transfer in place and press iron down firmly for about 30 seconds. Using this method, the design will be reversed; if you wish to use the design as shown, first trace onto paper with pencil, then retrace design on the wrong side with transfer pen before transferring to fabric.

Another transfer method employs the use of tulle or other open mesh fabric. Trace the design onto the tulle with a black fine-point permanent marker. Then place the tulle over the background fabric and retrace the lines with a pencil or removable pen. Enough of the design should transfer through the holes of the tulle for accurate stitching.

Stitching Tips & Techniques

When working with stranded threads like floss, always separate the strands then put together and realign the number of strands you wish to use. This is called stripping your floss.

If a needle is difficult to thread, turn it over so you are threading the opposite side of the hole; it may slip in more easily. You can also try inserting the other end of the thread into the needle.

If you will be working with different colors and kinds of threads, thread each into a needle before beginning your first stitch. Each new color will be readily available for stitching when you need it.

The neatest stitches are achieved by pulling the needle and thread completely through the fabric for each portion of the stitch.

Strive for consistent tension as you work. If you are trying a new stitch, practice a few rows on scrap fabric to establish a rhythm.

If a mistake is made, remove the needle from the thread and pick the work back to the error and restitch. If you try to "unstitch" the work with the needle you'll usually make a mess!

Finishing Notes

Wash your stitched piece in cool water, if needed. Wrap in a terry towel to remove moisture. Place face down on a dry towel or padded surface;

press carefully until dry. If not washing, dampen embroidery with a spritz of water before pressing.

12 Easy Stitches

1. Backstitch

Bring thread up at 1, a stitch length from beginning of design line. Stitch down at 2, at beginning of line. Come up at 3, stitch back down at 4 (same hole as 1). Continue in this manner, stitching backward to meet the previous stitch. Backstitch can be worked horizontally as shown, vertically, diagonally or along a curve.

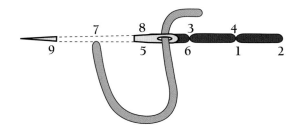

2. Wrapped Backstitch

Work a row of Backstitch. Bring a matching thread up at A, at beginning of line. Use an overcasting motion to pass needle downward beneath each backstitch without piercing fabric. Pull through consistently so each backstitch is loosely wrapped. Stitch down into fabric at end of backstitched line at B.

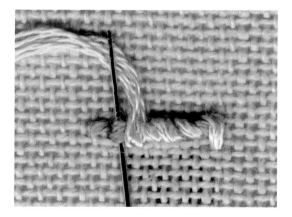

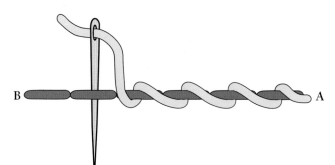

3. Blanket Stitch

This stitch is worked along imaginary lines. Bring needle up at 1 and make a counterclockwise loop. Stitch down at 2 (diagonally upward and to the right of 1) and up at 3 (directly below 2), keeping thread beneath point of needle. Pull through to form stitch and continue in this manner. The spacing between each stitch can vary depending on the area to be filled or the effect desired.

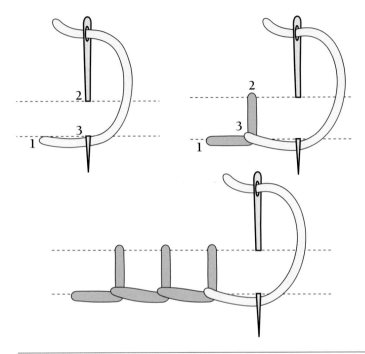

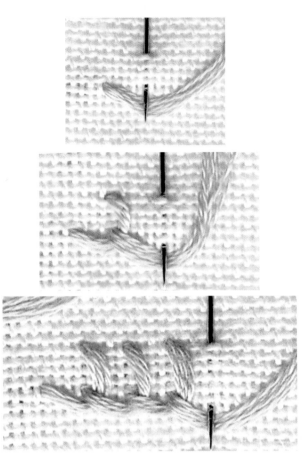

4. Chain Stitch

Bring thread up at 1. Form a counterclockwise loop and stitch down again at 2 (same hole as 1), holding loop with non-stitching thumb. Come up at 3, keeping loop beneath point of needle. Pull needle through, adjusting size and shape of loop. Repeat stitch to form a chain. End chain by stitching down over last loop at A. The chain can be worked horizontally, vertically, or along a curve.

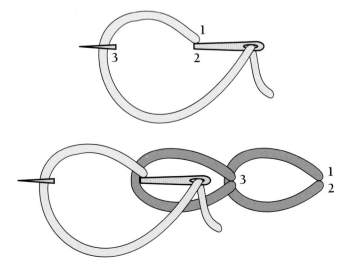

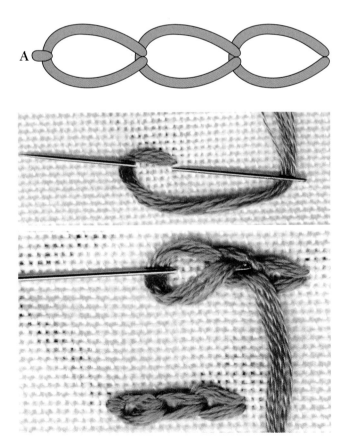

5. French Knot

Bring thread up at 1. Wrap thread once around shaft of needle. Insert needle down at 2 (close to, but at least one thread away from 1). Pull wrapping thread snug around needle and hold the thread as needle is pulled through wrap; release thread as knot tightens. For a larger French Knot, use more strands of thread.

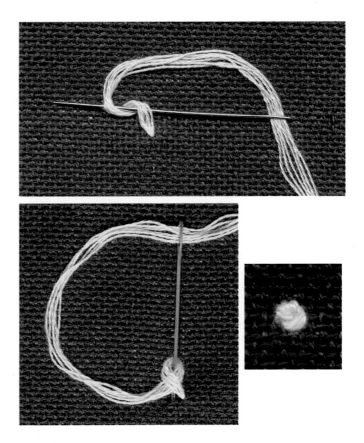

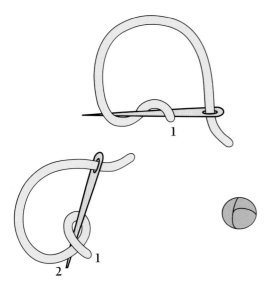

6. Fly Stitch

Bring thread up at 1 and swing thread to the right. Stitch down at 2 and up at 3 with the thread beneath point of needle; pull through, forming a V shape. Stitch down at 4. The stitches can be worked in rows (horizontal as shown or vertical) or in a random pattern.

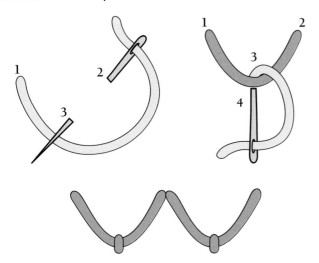

7. Lazy Daisy Stitch

Bring needle up at 1 and reinsert needle at 2 (same hole as 1). Bring needle up at 3 at desired length of loop, and pull thread until loop is formed. Stitch down over the loop at 4.

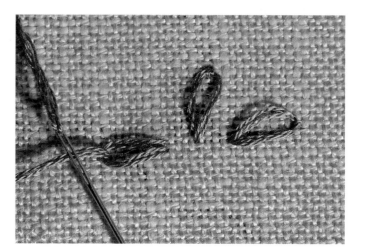

8. Running Stitch

Work stitches from right to left. Bring needle up at 1 and down at 2. Continue stitching, keeping length of stitches the same as the spaces between.

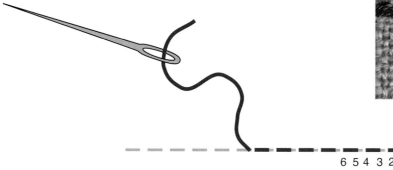

6 5 4 3 2 1

9. Satin Stitch

Follow the numerical sequence to work Straight Stitches next to each other to fill the desired space. Satin Stitch can be worked vertically, horizontally, or diagonally, and can be used to fill any desired shape. Do not make stitches too long or they might snag.

10. Smyrna Stitch

The Smyrna Stitch is a decorative stitch used to form a star. Follow the numbering to work the diagonal stitches first, and then stitch a cross on top.

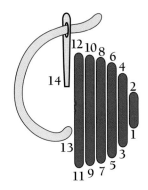

11. Stem Stitch

Bring thread up at 1, along the design line. Hold thread below line with the thumb of your non-stitching hand. Stitch down at 2 and up at 3 (half-way between 1 and 2); pull through. Continue in this manner with the working thread always below the design line. You can also work with the thread always above your work. Work straight or curved rows. When working on a tight curve, be sure the position of the working thread is on the outside of the curve.

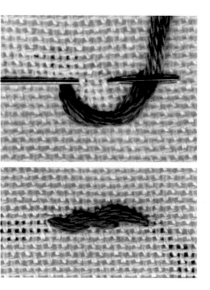

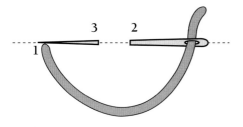

12. Straight Stitch

Bring thread up at 1 and down at 2. Straight Stitches can be worked in different directions, of varying sizes, and spaced as desired. Straight Stitches can be used to fill out or compensate in a small area composed of other stitches.

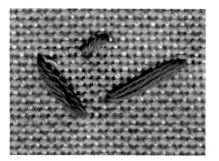

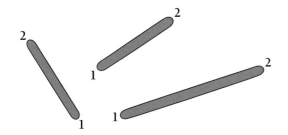

Top: Heart Greeting
Center: Windmill Card, Hot Air Balloon Card, Floral Note
Bottom: Heartstrings Card

Windmill Card

Materials:
- ¼ yd tan cotton fabric
- 4 x 5½-inch blank card
- Double-sided adhesive
- ½ yd of ⅜-inch gold trim
- Tacky craft glue or hot glue

Instructions

1. Cut 3½ x 4½-inch rectangle from tan fabric. (If using embroidery hoop, cut rectangle large enough to fit.)
2. Transfer design to tan rectangle. *(See Transfer Techniques on page 6.)*
3. Embroider design referring to diagram and photograph for stitches and floss colors.
4. Cut four ¾-inch squares of double sided adhesive. Peel protective paper from one side of adhesive and attach it to wrong side of embroidered design at each corner.
5. Remove remaining protective paper and attach the embroidered rectangle to the card.
6. Cut two 3½-inch and two 4½-inch lengths of trim.
7. Glue trim to card around edges of embroidered fabric.

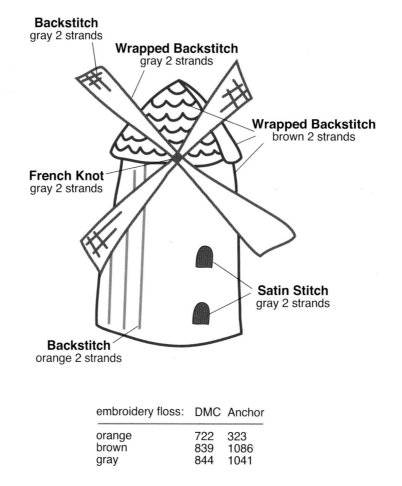

Backstitch
gray 2 strands

Wrapped Backstitch
gray 2 strands

Wrapped Backstitch
brown 2 strands

French Knot
gray 2 strands

Satin Stitch
gray 2 strands

Backstitch
orange 2 strands

embroidery floss:	DMC	Anchor
orange	722	323
brown	839	1086
gray	844	1041

Hot Air Balloon Card

Materials
- ¼ yd tan cotton fabric
- 4 x 5½-inch blank card
- Double-sided adhesive
- ½ yd of ⅜-inch wide gold trim
- Tacky craft glue or hot glue

Instructions
1. Cut 3½ x 4½-inch rectangle from tan fabric. (If using embroidery hoop, cut squares large enough to fit.)
2. Transfer design to tan rectangle. *(See Transfer Techniques on page 6.)*
3. Embroider design referring to diagram and photograph for stitches and floss colors.
4. Cut four ¾-inch squares of double sided adhesive. Peel protective paper from one side of adhesive and attach it to wrong side of embroidered design at each corner.
5. Remove remaining protective paper and attach the embroidered rectangle to the card.
6. Cut two 3½-inch and two 4½-inch lengths of trim.
7. Glue trim to card around edges of embroidered fabric.

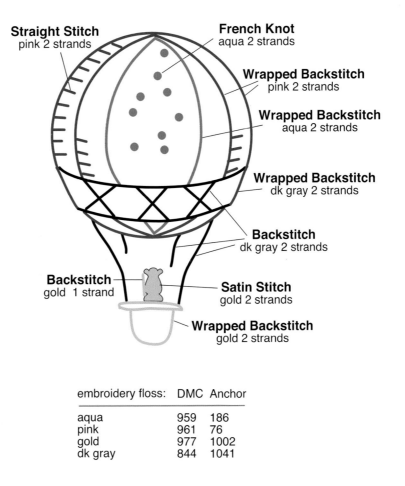

Straight Stitch pink 2 strands

French Knot aqua 2 strands

Wrapped Backstitch pink 2 strands

Wrapped Backstitch aqua 2 strands

Wrapped Backstitch dk gray 2 strands

Backstitch dk gray 2 strands

Backstitch gold 1 strand

Satin Stitch gold 2 strands

Wrapped Backstitch gold 2 strands

embroidery floss:	DMC	Anchor
aqua	959	186
pink	961	76
gold	977	1002
dk gray	844	1041

Heartstrings Card

Materials
- ¼ yd blue cotton fabric
- 5½ x 4-inch blank card
- Double-sided adhesive
- ½ yd medium wide multi-color rickrack
- Tacky craft glue or hot glue

Instructions
1. Cut 5 x 3½-inch rectangle from blue fabric. (If using embroidery hoop, cut rectangle large enough to fit.)
2. Transfer design to blue rectangle. *(See Transfer Techniques on page 6.)*
3. Embroider design referring to diagram and photograph for stitches and floss colors.
4. Cut four ¾-inch squares of double-sided adhesive. Peel protective paper from one side of adhesive and attach it to wrong side of embroidered design at each corner.
5. Remove remaining protective paper and attach the embroidered rectangle to the card.
6. Cut two 3¾-inch and two 5-inch lengths of trim.
7. Glue trim to card around edges of embroidered fabric, overlapping corners.

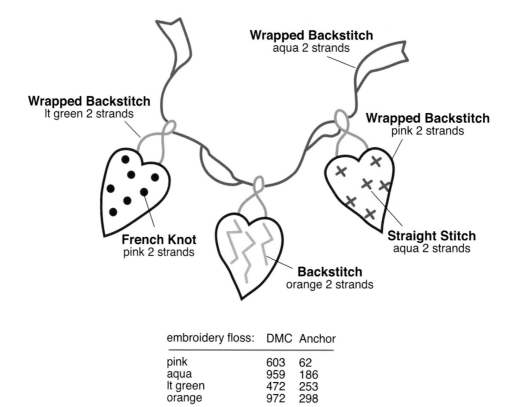

Wrapped Backstitch
aqua 2 strands

Wrapped Backstitch
lt green 2 strands

Wrapped Backstitch
pink 2 strands

French Knot
pink 2 strands

Straight Stitch
aqua 2 strands

Backstitch
orange 2 strands

embroidery floss:	DMC	Anchor
pink	603	62
aqua	959	186
lt green	472	253
orange	972	298

Floral Note

Materials
- ¼ yd beige print fabric
- 5 x 7-inch blank card
- 4 x 4½-inch card stock
- 32 rocaille green seed beads, 4mm
- Tacky craft glue or hot glue

Instructions

1. Cut 5½ x 6-inch rectangle from beige print fabric. (If using embroidery hoop, cut rectangle large enough to fit.)

2. Transfer design to center of fabric. *(See Transfer Techniques on page 6.)*

3. Embroider design referring to diagram and photograph for stitches and floss colors.

4. Stretch embroidered fabric over card stock. Fold edges to back, folding corners in; glue fabric in place at top and sides of card stock. Do not glue lower edge yet.

5. Fold bottom edge of fabric over card, forming crease. Sew beads to fabric along crease as follows: For the fringes, string eight beads onto thread; bring needle back up through seven beads skipping lowest bead; thread both ends into needle and sew to crease ¼ inch from the left edge. Repeat two more times, at ¼-inch intervals. Sew remaining single beads at ¼-inch intervals.

6. Glue fabric in place at bottom of card stock with beads hanging below bottom edge.

7. Glue embroidered fabric to card at a slight angle.

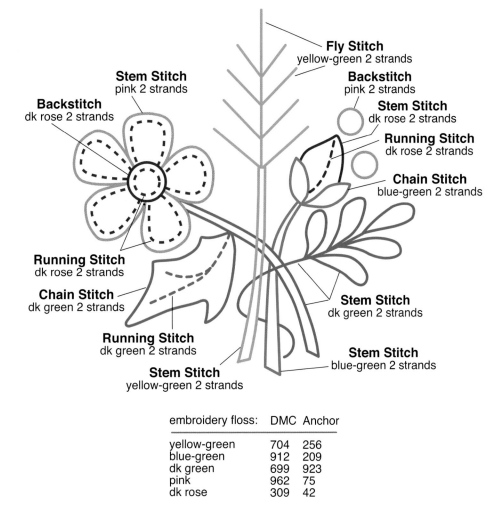

embroidery floss:	DMC	Anchor
yellow-green	704	256
blue-green	912	209
dk green	699	923
pink	962	75
dk rose	309	42

Heart Greeting

Materials
- ¼ yd pink fabric
- 14 iridescent rose seed beads, 3mm
- 3 ⅞-inch square card stock
- 5 x 7-inch blank card
- Tacky craft glue or hot glue

Instructions

1. Cut 5½-inch square from pink fabric. (If using embroidery hoop, cut square large enough to fit.)
2. Transfer design to center of pink square. *(See Transfer Techniques on page 6.)*
3. Embroider design referring to diagram and photograph for stitches and floss colors.
4. Sew beads to fabric with 2 strands of floss along inside of heart according to diagram. Sew single bead in center of flower with 2 strands of floss.
5. Stretch embroidered fabric over card stock, folding corners in; glue in place.
6. Referring to photo on page 13, sew four corner beads in place.
7. Glue embroidery square onto card at a slight angle.

Stem Stitch yellow-green 2 strands
Stem Stitch bright green 2 strands
Stem Stitch bright green 2 strands
bead placement
Chain Stitch rose 2 strands
Chain Stitch lt pink 2 strands
Fly Stitch bright green 2 strands
Straight Stitch red 1 strand
Stem Stitch yellow-green 2 strands
French Knot yellow 2 strands
Lazy Daisy yellow-green 2 strands
Lazy Daisy bright green 2 strands

embroidery floss:	DMC	Anchor
yellow	3821	305
yellow-green	3348	264
bright green	704	256
lt pink	894	27
rose	962	75
red	321	9046

Top: Box in Bloom, Butterfly Box
Bottom: Woodland Leaves, Paisleys & Posies

Butterfly Box

Materials

- Turquoise acrylic paint
- Paint sponge
- 4½-inch square gift box
- ¼ yd ivory fabric
- Mat board, cardboard or foamcore to fit top of box
- 4½-inch square of cotton batting
- 20 inches of ½-inch dk green braid
- Tacky craft glue or hot glue

Instructions

1. Paint gift box, using sponge.
2. Cut 6-inch square from ivory fabric. (If using embroidery hoop, cut square large enough to fit.)
3. Transfer pattern to fabric. (*See Transfer Techniques on page 6.*)
4. Embroider design referring to diagram and photograph for stitches and floss colors.
5. Cut mat board, cardboard or foamcore to fit top of box.

6. Lightly glue batting to board or foamcore.
7. Stretch embroidered fabric over batting and board, fold in corners and sides, and pin to hold in place.
8. Glue embroidered fabric to back of padded board. Remove pins.
9. Glue board to box cover.
10. Glue braid around edge of box cover.

embroidery floss:	DMC	Anchor
pink	3804	63
orange	972	298
dk brown	839	1086
lt green	3348	264
green	3346	267
aqua	992	1072

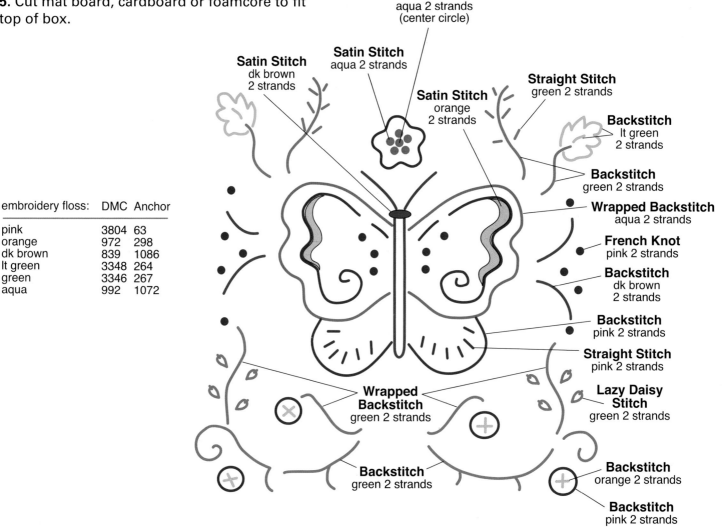

French Knot aqua 2 strands (center circle)

Satin Stitch aqua 2 strands

Satin Stitch dk brown 2 strands

Satin Stitch orange 2 strands

Straight Stitch green 2 strands

Backstitch lt green 2 strands

Backstitch green 2 strands

Wrapped Backstitch aqua 2 strands

French Knot pink 2 strands

Backstitch dk brown 2 strands

Backstitch pink 2 strands

Straight Stitch pink 2 strands

Lazy Daisy Stitch green 2 strands

Wrapped Backstitch green 2 strands

Backstitch green 2 strands

Backstitch orange 2 strands

Backstitch pink 2 strands

Box in Bloom

Materials

- Dark green acrylic paint
- Paint sponge
- 4½-inch square gift box
- ¼ yd lt green print fabric
- Mat board, cardboard or foamcore to fit top of box
- 4 ½-inch square of cotton batting
- 20 inches of ¼-inch dk green braid
- Tacky craft glue or hot glue

Instructions

1. Paint gift box, using sponge.
2. Cut 6-inch square from lt green fabric. (If using embroidery hoop, cut square large enough to fit.)
3. Transfer design to fabric. *(See Transfer Techniques on page 6.)*
4. Embroider design referring to diagram and photograph for stitches and floss colors.

5. Cut mat board, cardboard or foamcore to fit top of box.
6. Lightly glue batting to board or foamcore.
7. Stretch embroidered fabric over batting and board, fold in corners and sides, and pin to hold in place.
8. Glue embroidered fabric to back of padded board. Remove pins.
9. Glue board to box cover.
10. Glue braid around edge of box cover.

Stem Stitch
turquoise 2 strands

Straight Stitch
black 2 strands

Stem Stitch
yellow-green 2 strands

Straight Stitch
yellow-green 2 strands

Chain Stitch
yellow-green 2 strands

Straight Stitch
black 2 strands

Stem Stitch
blue-green 2 strands

Stem Stitch
blue 2 strands

Stem Stitch
med green 2 strands

Stem Stitch
yellow-green 2 strands

Stem Stitch
blue-green 2 strands

French Knot
yellow 2 strands

Straight Stitch
med green 2 strands

Stem Stitch
med green 2 strands

Stem Stitch
lavender 2 strands

French Knot
yellow-green 2 strands

Straight Stitch
black 2 strands

Chain Stitch
yellow-green 2 strands

Stem Stitch
yellow-green 2 strands

embroidery floss:	DMC	Anchor
yellow	743	302
yellow-green	704	256
med green	701	227
blue-green	912	209
turquoise	3846	167
blue	517	162
lavender	155	118
black	310	403

Paisleys & Posies

Materials

- Brick red acrylic paint
- Paint sponge
- 4½-inch diameter round gift box
- ¼ yd pink fabric
- Mat board, cardboard or foamcore to fit top of box
- 4¼-inch square of cotton batting
- 18 inches of ½-inch pink braid
- 24 dk rose iridescent seed beads, 3mm
- 9 green rocaille seed beads, 4mm
- Tacky craft glue or hot glue

Instructions

1. Paint gift box, using sponge.

2. Cut 5-inch square from pink fabric. (If using embroidery hoop, cut square large enough to fit.)

3. Transfer pattern to pink square. *(See Transfer Techniques on page 6.)*

4. Embroider design referring to diagram and photograph for stitches and floss colors. On rust colored Lazy Daisy stitches, attach a dk rose bead on the stitch that secures the loop.

5. Sew green beads in centers of small flowers, using 2 strands of peach floss.

6. Cut mat board, cardboard or foamcore to fit top of box.

7. Lightly glue batting to board or foamcore.

8. Stretch embroidered fabric over batting and board, fold in corners and sides, and pin to hold in place.

9. Glue embroidered fabric to back of padded board. Remove pins.

10. Glue board to box cover.

11. Glue braid around edge of box cover.

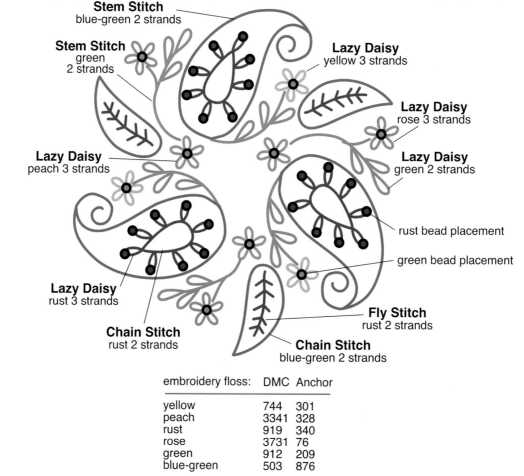

Stem Stitch
blue-green 2 strands

Stem Stitch
green 2 strands

Lazy Daisy
peach 3 strands

Lazy Daisy
rust 3 strands

Chain Stitch
rust 2 strands

Lazy Daisy
yellow 3 strands

Lazy Daisy
rose 3 strands

Lazy Daisy
green 2 strands

rust bead placement

green bead placement

Fly Stitch
rust 2 strands

Chain Stitch
blue-green 2 strands

embroidery floss:	DMC	Anchor
yellow	744	301
peach	3341	328
rust	919	340
rose	3731	76
green	912	209
blue-green	503	876

Woodland Leaves

Materials
- Purple acrylic paint
- Paint sponge
- 2½-inch square gift box
- ¼ yd turquoise fabric
- Mat board, cardboard or foamcore to fit top of box
- 2¼-inch square of cotton batting
- 12 inches of ¼-inch metallic gold braid
- Tacky craft glue or hot glue

Instructions
1. Paint gift box, using sponge.
2. Cut 3¾-inch square from turquoise fabric. (If using embroidery hoop, cut square large enough to fit.)
3. Transfer pattern to turquoise square. *(See Transfer Techniques on page 6.)*
4. Embroider design referring to diagram and photograph for stitches and floss colors.
5. Cut mat board, cardboard or foamcore to fit top of box.
6. Lightly glue batting to board or foamcore.
7. Stretch embroidered fabric over batting and board, fold in corners and sides, and pin to hold in place.
8. Glue embroidered fabric to back of padded board. Remove pins.
9. Glue board to box cover.
10. Glue braid around edge of box cover.

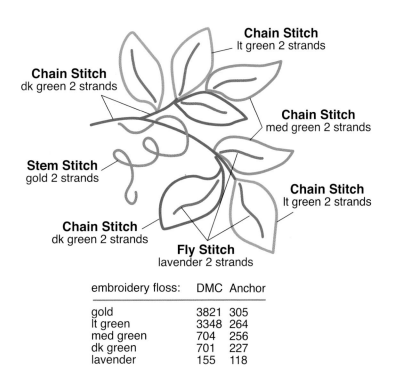

Chain Stitch
lt green 2 strands

Chain Stitch
dk green 2 strands

Chain Stitch
med green 2 strands

Stem Stitch
gold 2 strands

Chain Stitch
lt green 2 strands

Chain Stitch
dk green 2 strands

Fly Stitch
lavender 2 strands

embroidery floss:	DMC	Anchor
gold	3821	305
lt green	3348	264
med green	704	256
dk green	701	227
lavender	155	118

Blooming Bulb Towels

Blooming Bulb Towels

Materials
- ¼ yd beige print cotton fabric
- ⅛ yd navy print cotton
- Two cotton dish towels

Instructions
1. Cut two 5½ x 6-inch rectangles from beige fabric. (If using embroidery hoop, cut rectangles large enough to fit.)
2. Transfer one flower design onto each rectangle. *(See Transfer Techniques on page 6.)*
3. Embroider design referring to diagram and photograph for stitches and floss colors.
4. Cut two ¾ x 6-inch strips and two ¾ x 7-inch strips

from navy fabric. With right sides together, stitch to top, bottom and sides of embroidered rectangle with a ¼-inch seam. Press seam toward border.
5. Press raw edges under. Pin rectangle to towels and stitch close to edge with zigzag stitch.

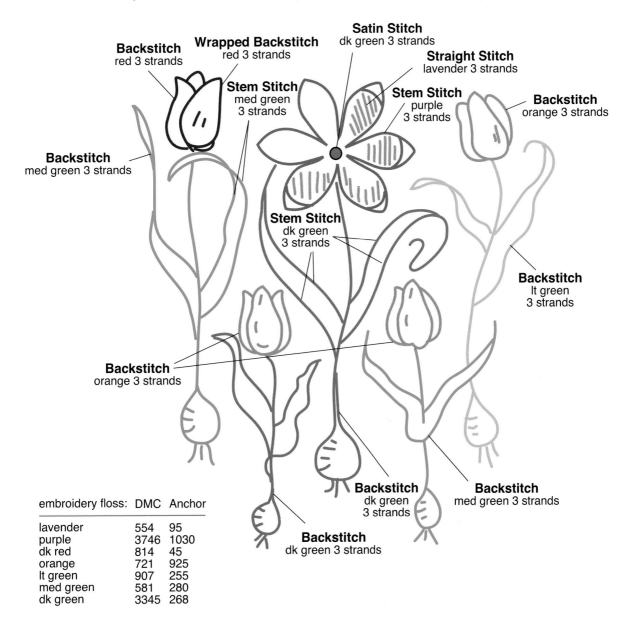

embroidery floss:	DMC	Anchor
lavender	554	95
purple	3746	1030
dk red	814	45
orange	721	925
lt green	907	255
med green	581	280
dk green	3345	268

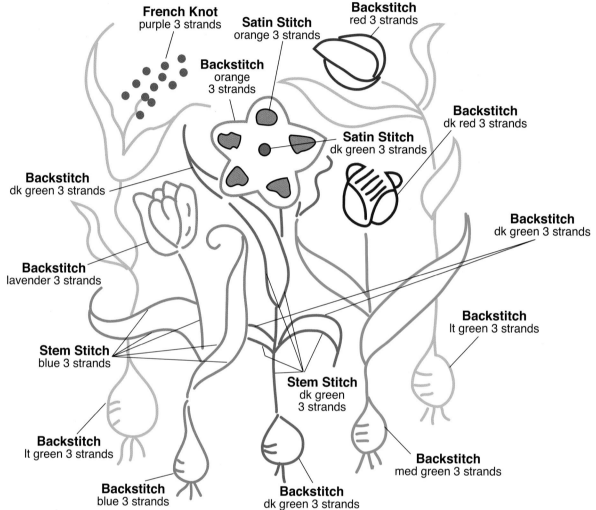

French Knot
purple 3 strands

Satin Stitch
orange 3 strands

Backstitch
red 3 strands

Backstitch
orange
3 strands

Backstitch
dk red 3 strands

Satin Stitch
dk green 3 strands

Backstitch
dk green 3 strands

Backstitch
dk green 3 strands

Backstitch
lavender 3 strands

Backstitch
lt green 3 strands

Stem Stitch
blue 3 strands

Stem Stitch
dk green
3 strands

Backstitch
lt green 3 strands

Backstitch
blue 3 strands

Backstitch
dk green 3 strands

Backstitch
med green 3 strands

embroidery floss:	DMC	Anchor
lavender	554	95
purple	3746	1030
dk red	814	45
red	817	13
orange	721	925
lt green	907	255
med green	581	280
dk green	3345	268
blue	518	1039

Top: Star Flowers
Bottom: Sunshine Flower, Queen Anne Sachet

Sunshine Flower

Materials

- 5½ x 8-inch journal
- 4½ x 6½-inch piece blue felt
- 1-inch diameter circle of lt yellow felt
- 3-inch square piece of dk yellow felt
- 1 x 6-inch piece of lt green felt
- ½ x 4-inch piece of dk green felt
- 16 black beads, 2mm
- 12 inches of 1½-inch wide black and white ribbon or ribbon of your choice
- Iron-on transfer pen
- Tacky craft glue or hot glue

Instructions

1. Transfer design onto blue rectangle. *(See Transfer Techniques on page 6.)*

2. Cut flower center from lt yellow felt referring to diagram.

3. Cut flower from dk yellow felt referring to diagram.

4. Cut flower stem from dk green felt referring to diagram.

5. Cut leaves from lt green felt referring to diagram.

6. Embroider felt pieces referring to diagram and photograph for stitches and floss colors.

7. Sew beads to flower center, referring to diagram for placement.

8. Glue center to flower. Glue flower, stem and leaves to blue felt.

9. Embroider running stitch around petals as shown in diagram.

10. Place ribbon along edge of journal binding, with ends wrapping to inside front cover. Glue in place.

11. Center embroidered felt on journal and glue in place.

embroidery floss:	DMC	Anchor
red	3801	35
yellow	445	288
bright green	704	256
dk green	319	218

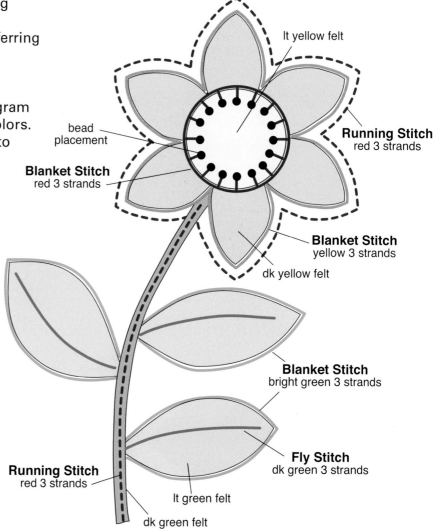

It yellow felt

Running Stitch
red 3 strands

bead placement

Blanket Stitch
red 3 strands

Blanket Stitch
yellow 3 strands

dk yellow felt

Blanket Stitch
bright green 3 strands

Fly Stitch
dk green 3 strands

Running Stitch
red 3 strands

It green felt

dk green felt

Star Flowers

Materials
- 5½ x 8-inch journal
- ¼ yd purple felt
- Iron-on transfer pen
- 16-inch piece of 1-inch wide blue ribbon
- Tacky craft glue or hot glue

Instructions
1. Cut 5 x 6 ½-inch rectangle from purple felt. (If using embroidery hoop, cut rectangle large enough to fit.)
2. Transfer design onto rectangle. *(See Transfer Techniques on page 6.)*
3. Embroider design referring to diagram and photograph for stitches and floss colors.

4. Place ribbon along left side of journal, ½ inch from edge, with ends wrapping to inside of front cover. Glue in place.
5. Center embroidered felt on journal and glue in place.

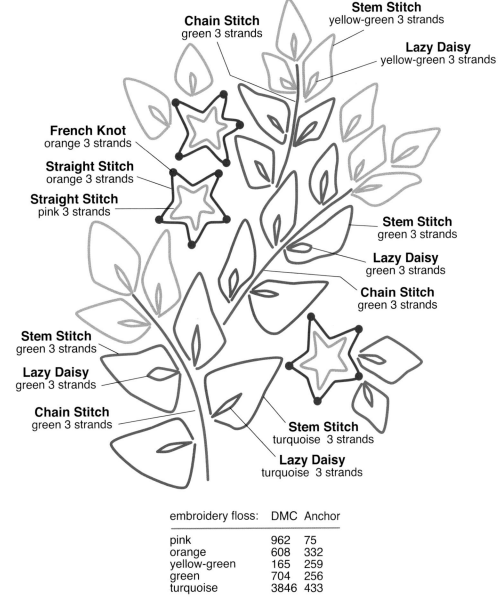

Chain Stitch
green 3 strands

Stem Stitch
yellow-green 3 strands

Lazy Daisy
yellow-green 3 strands

French Knot
orange 3 strands

Straight Stitch
orange 3 strands

Straight Stitch
pink 3 strands

Stem Stitch
green 3 strands

Lazy Daisy
green 3 strands

Chain Stitch
green 3 strands

Stem Stitch
green 3 strands

Lazy Daisy
green 3 strands

Chain Stitch
green 3 strands

Stem Stitch
turquoise 3 strands

Lazy Daisy
turquoise 3 strands

embroidery floss:	DMC	Anchor
pink	962	75
orange	608	332
yellow-green	165	259
green	704	256
turquoise	3846	433

Queen Anne Sachet

Materials
- ¼ yd yellow felt
- Polyester fiberfill or potpourri
- 1 yd green piping, ½-inch wide

Instructions
1. Cut two 5-inch squares from yellow felt. (If using embroidery hoop, cut squares large enough to fit.)
2. Transfer design to center of one yellow square. *(See Transfer Techniques on page 6.)*
3. Embroider design referring to diagram and photograph for stitches and floss colors.
4. Position piping ¼ inch from edge of sachet front at the middle of the sachet front, leaving a

2-inch piece of piping free. Stitch close to piping with a zipper foot, overlapping a 2-inch end piece over the beginning piece.
5. With wrong sides together, sew raw edges of the two squares of felt together, leaving a 2-inch opening.
6. Fill with fiberfill or potpourri; stitch opening closed.

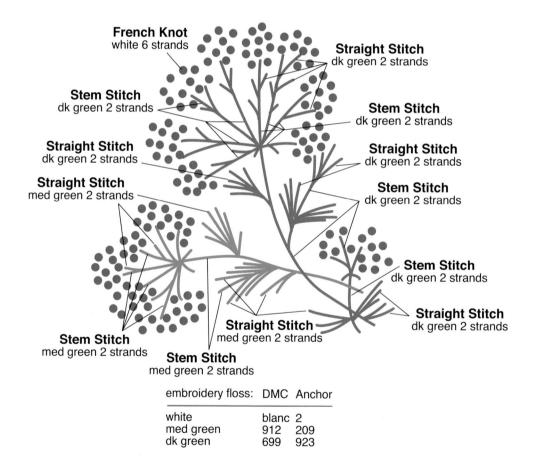

French Knot
white 6 strands

Straight Stitch
dk green 2 strands

Stem Stitch
dk green 2 strands

Stem Stitch
dk green 2 strands

Straight Stitch
dk green 2 strands

Straight Stitch
dk green 2 strands

Straight Stitch
med green 2 strands

Stem Stitch
dk green 2 strands

Stem Stitch
dk green 2 strands

Stem Stitch
dk green 2 strands

Straight Stitch
dk green 2 strands

Straight Stitch
med green 2 strands

Stem Stitch
med green 2 strands

Stem Stitch
med green 2 strands

embroidery floss:	DMC	Anchor
white	blanc	2
med green	912	209
dk green	699	923

Top: Stylized Bouquet
Bottom: Botanical Ranunculas

Botanical Ranunculus

Materials
- ¼ yd cotton
- 8 x 10-inch mat board with 6 x 7½-inch opening
- 8 x 10-inch frame
- 8 x 10-inch piece of backing board or foam core
- Tacky craft glue or hot glue

Instructions
1. Cut 10 x 12-inch rectangle from cotton muslin. (If using embroidery hoop, cut piece large enough to fit.)
2. Transfer design on page 33 to rectangle. *(See Transfer Techniques on page 6.)*
3. Embroider design referring to diagram and photograph for stitches and floss colors.
4. Place finished embroidered piece on backing board or foam core. Stretch over sides and pin to secure temporarily.

5. Trim edges to 1 inch outside of backing board or foam core. Turn edges to back and glue in place. Remove pins.
6. Place mat board over stitched piece and place in frame.

Stylized Bouquet

Materials
- ¼ yd cotton
- 8 x 10-inch mat board with 5 x 7-inch opening
- 8 x 10-inch frame
- 8 x 10-inch piece of backing board or foam core
- Tacky craft glue or hot glue

Instructions
1. Cut 10 x 12-inch rectangle from cotton muslin. (If using embroidery hoop, cut rectangle large enough to fit.)
2. Transfer design on page 34 to rectangle. *(See Transfer Techniques on page 6.)*
3. Embroider design referring to diagram and photograph for stitches and floss colors.
4. Place finished embroidered piece on backing board or foam core. Stretch

over sides and pin to secure temporarily.
5. Trim edges to 1 inch outside of backing board or foam core. Turn edges to back and glue in place. Remove pins.
6. Place mat board over stitched piece and place in frame.

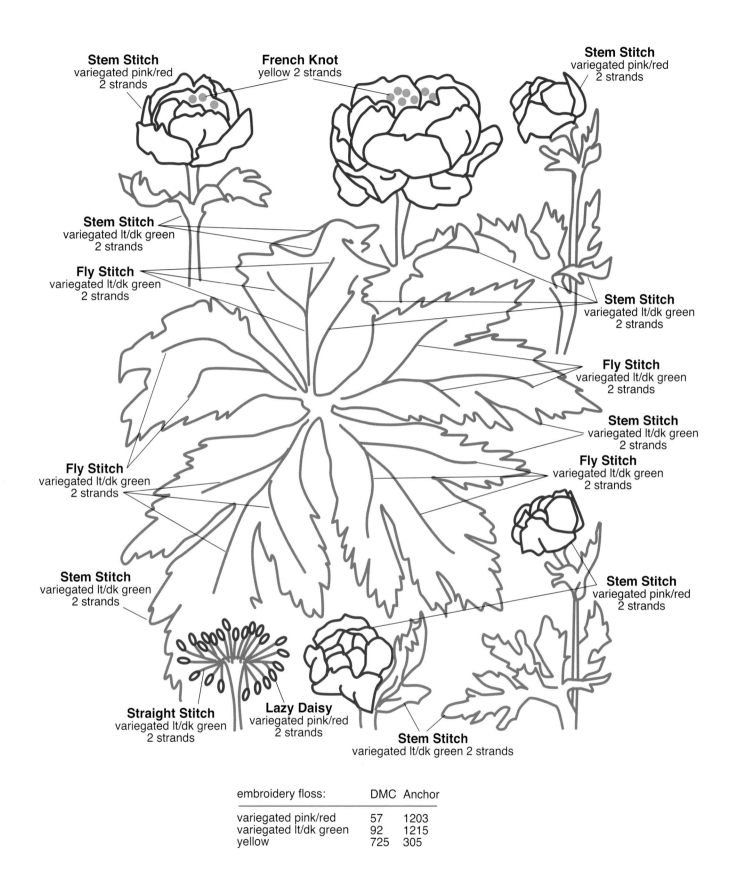

Stem Stitch
variegated pink/red
2 strands

French Knot
yellow 2 strands

Stem Stitch
variegated pink/red
2 strands

Stem Stitch
variegated lt/dk green
2 strands

Fly Stitch
variegated lt/dk green
2 strands

Stem Stitch
variegated lt/dk green
2 strands

Fly Stitch
variegated lt/dk green
2 strands

Stem Stitch
variegated lt/dk green
2 strands

Fly Stitch
variegated lt/dk green
2 strands

Fly Stitch
variegated lt/dk green
2 strands

Stem Stitch
variegated lt/dk green
2 strands

Stem Stitch
variegated pink/red
2 strands

Straight Stitch
variegated lt/dk green
2 strands

Lazy Daisy
variegated pink/red
2 strands

Stem Stitch
variegated lt/dk green 2 strands

embroidery floss:	DMC	Anchor
variegated pink/red	57	1203
variegated lt/dk green	92	1215
yellow	725	305

Chain Stitch
dk rose 2 strands

Chain Stitch
purple 2 strands

Straight Stitch
peach 2 strands

Blanket Stitch
bright green 2 strands

Stem Stitch
dk rose 2 strands

Straight Stitch
peach 2 strands

French Knot
bright green 2 strands

Stem Stitch
turquoise 2 strands

Chain Stitch
bright green 2 strands

Chain Stitch
purple 2 strands

Chain Stitch
turquoise 2 strands

Chain Stitch
dk rose 2 strands

Stem Stitch
purple 2 strands

Chain Stitch
peach 2 strands

Stem Stitch
turquoise 2 strands

Chain Stitch
bright green 2 strands

embroidery floss:	DMC	Anchor
purple	333	119
dk rose	3803	69
peach	352	9
bright green	704	256
turquoise	959	186

Top: Fetching Puppy Patch
Bottom: Sail Away Pillow

Fetching Puppy Patch

Materials
- ¼ yd lt yellow cotton fabric
- ¼ yd white flannel
- Denim jacket or your choice of garment
- 1 yd of ½-inch wide trim of your choice

Instructions
1. Cut 4 x 5-inch rectangle from yellow fabric. (If using embroidery hoop, cut rectangle large enough to fit.)
2. Transfer design to yellow rectangle. *(See Transfer Techniques on page 6.)*
3. Embroider design referring to diagram and photograph for stitches and floss colors.
4. Cut rectangle from white flannel ½-inch larger than embroidered rectangle.
5. Pin flannel rectangle to garment. Pin embroidered rectangle to flannel rectangle. Stitch through all layers around outside edges.
6. Stitch trim along both sides of rectangle, then along top and bottom of rectangle, folding ends in.

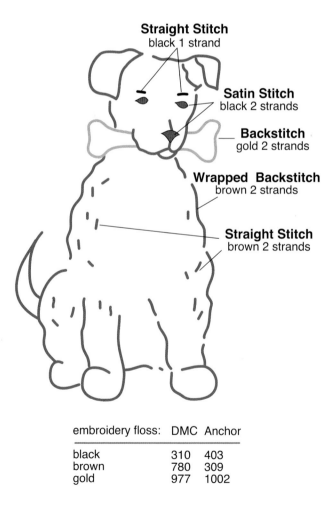

Straight Stitch
black 1 strand

Satin Stitch
black 2 strands

Backstitch
gold 2 strands

Wrapped Backstitch
brown 2 strands

Straight Stitch
brown 2 strands

embroidery floss:	DMC	Anchor
black	310	403
brown	780	309
gold	977	1002

Sail Away Pillow

Materials
- ¼ yd white cotton fabric
- ⅛ yd blue cotton fabric
- 9½-inch length star trim or trim of your choice
- ⅓ yd cotton backing fabric
- Polyester fiberfill

Instructions
1. Cut 4¼ x 5¼-inch rectangle from white fabric. (If using embroidery hoop, cut rectangle large enough to fit.)
2. Transfer sailboat design onto white rectangle. *(See Transfer Techniques on page 6.)*
3. Embroider design referring to diagram and photograph for stitches and floss colors.
4. Cut two 4¼ x 3-inch rectangles from blue fabric.
5. Stitch blue rectangles to top and bottom of embroidered rectangle. Press seams toward blue fabric.
6. Cut two 3 x 10¼-inch strips from blue fabric.

Stitch strips to sides of the pieced section. Press seams toward blue fabric.
7. Stitch trim to pillow ¼ inch below embroidered rectangle.
8. Cut one 9¼ x 10¼-inch rectangle from backing fabric. With right sides together, stitch pillow front to backing fabric, leaving a 5-inch opening to allow for turning.
9. Trim excess fabric from corners. Turn right side out, insert fiberfill and slipstitch opening closed.

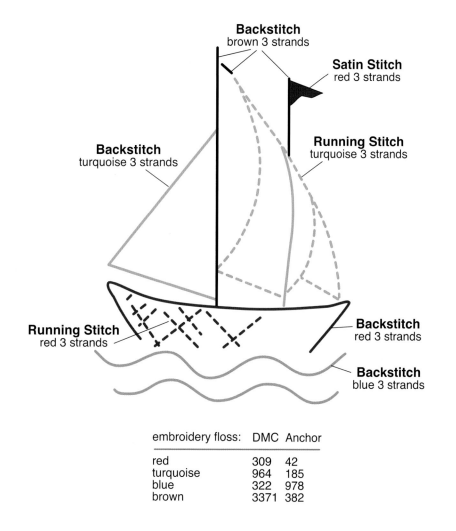

Backstitch
brown 3 strands

Satin Stitch
red 3 strands

Backstitch
turquoise 3 strands

Running Stitch
turquoise 3 strands

Running Stitch
red 3 strands

Backstitch
red 3 strands

Backstitch
blue 3 strands

embroidery floss:	DMC	Anchor
red	309	42
turquoise	964	185
blue	322	978
brown	3371	382

Top: Spring Songbird Pillow
Bottom: Apple Blossom Pillow, Floral Vase Pillow

Blossom Pillow

bric and
ric. (If using
gh to fit.)
e. *(See*

am and
s.
es to
ating
¼-inch

pink fabric.

With right sides together, stitch strips to top and bottom of patchwork square. Press seams open.
7. Cut two 1½ x 12½-inch strips from lt pink fabric. With right sides together, stitch strips to sides of the pieced square. Press seams open.
8. For pillow back, cut square from lt pink fabric the same size as the pillow front. With right sides together, stitch to pillow front, leaving a 6-inch opening to allow for turning.
9. Trim excess fabric from corners. Turn right side out, insert pillow and slipstitch opening closed.

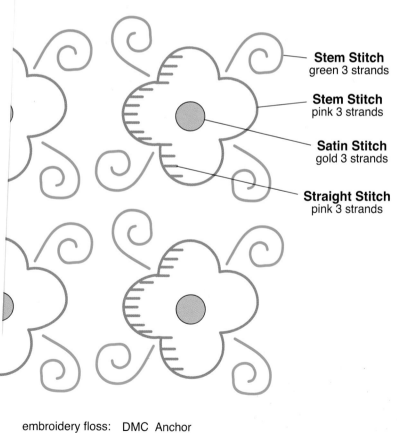

Stem Stitch
green 3 strands

Stem Stitch
pink 3 strands

Satin Stitch
gold 3 strands

Straight Stitch
pink 3 strands

embroidery floss:	DMC	Anchor
green	3346	267
gold	977	1002
pink	3804	63

Floral Vase Pillow

Materials
- ¼ yd white cotton fabric
- ½ yd green print cotton fabric
- ½ yd white flannel
- ½ yd cotton backing fabric
- 12-inch pillow insert

Instructions
1. Transfer design to white fabric. *(See Transfer Techniques on page 6.)*

2. Embroider design referring to diagram and photograph for stitches and floss color. Trim around design, leaving a ¾-inch margin around vase and flowers.

3. Cut one 12½-inch square from green fabric. Pin embroidered design to center of green square and zigzag stitch around outside edge.

4. Cut one 12½-inch square from flannel fabric. Place green square, right side up, on flannel square. Stitch diagonal lines through both layers of fabric, but not through embroidered piece.

5. Cut one 12½-inch

square from backing fabric. With right sides together, stitch pillow front to backing fabric, leaving a 6-inch opening to allow for turning.

6. Turn right side out, insert pillow and slipstitch opening closed.

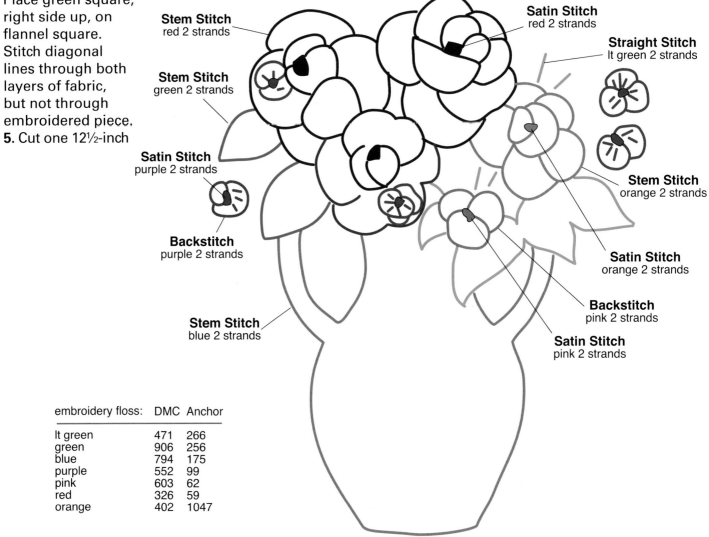

Stem Stitch
red 2 strands

Satin Stitch
red 2 strands

Straight Stitch
lt green 2 strands

Stem Stitch
green 2 strands

Satin Stitch
purple 2 strands

Stem Stitch
orange 2 strands

Backstitch
purple 2 strands

Satin Stitch
orange 2 strands

Backstitch
pink 2 strands

Stem Stitch
blue 2 strands

Satin Stitch
pink 2 strands

embroidery floss:	DMC	Anchor
lt green	471	266
green	906	256
blue	794	175
purple	552	99
pink	603	62
red	326	59
orange	402	1047

Spring Songbird Pillow

Materials

- ¼ yd ivory cotton fabric
- ⅛ yd lt blue cotton fabric
- ⅛ yd dk blue cotton fabric
- ⅛ yd turquoise print fabric
- ⅓ yd cotton backing fabric
- Polyester fiberfill

Instructions

1. Cut two 4-inch squares from ivory fabric. (If using embroidery hoop, cut squares large enough to fit.)

2. Transfer bird design onto one square and wreath design onto the other. *(See Transfer Techniques on page 6.)*

3. Embroider designs referring to diagram and photograph for stitches and floss colors.

4. Cut two 4 x 8-inch rectangles from ivory fabric. (If using embroidery hoop, cut rectangles large enough to fit.)

5. Transfer morning glory design onto each rectangle.

6. Embroider design referring to diagram and photograph for stitches and floss colors.

7. Cut one 1 x 4-inch strip from lt blue fabric.

8. Stitch strip between bottom of bird square and top of wreath square **(Fig 1)**. Press seams toward blue fabric.

9. Cut two 1 x 8-inch strips from lt blue fabric.

10. Stitch strips to sides of pieced rectangle **(Fig 2)**. Press. Stitch morning glory rectangles to sides of pieced rectangle **(Fig 3)**. Press seams toward blue fabric.

13. Cut two 1 x 13-inch strips from turquoise fabric. Stitch to top and bottom of pieced rectangle. Press.

14. Cut two 1 x 10-inch strips from turquoise fabric. Stitch to sides of pieced rectangle. Press.

15. Cut one 10 x 14-inch rectangle from backing fabric. With right sides together, stitch pillow front to backing fabric, leaving a 6-inch opening to allow for turning.

16. Trim excess fabric from corners. Turn right side out, insert fiberfill and slipstitch opening closed.

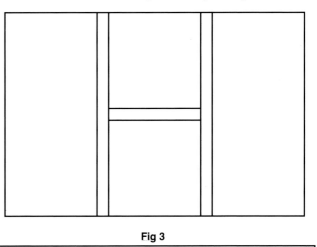

Fig 3

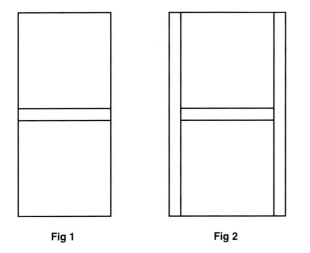

Fig 1   Fig 2

11. Cut two 1 x 8-inch strips from dk blue fabric. Stitch to sides of pieced rectangle **(Fig 4)**. Press.

12. Cut two 1 x 13-inch strips from dk blue fabric. Stitch to top and bottom of pieced rectangle. Press.

Fig 4

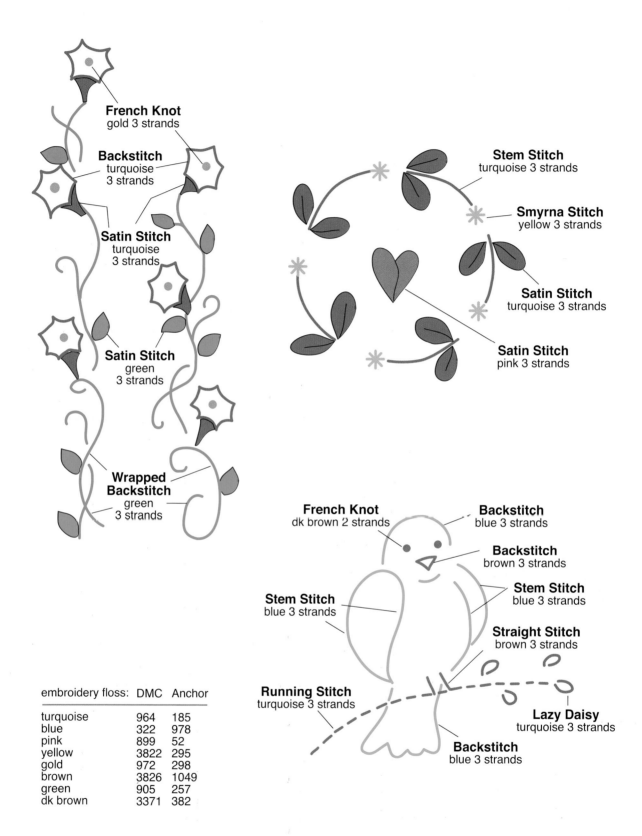

French Knot
gold 3 strands

Backstitch
turquoise
3 strands

Satin Stitch
turquoise
3 strands

Satin Stitch
green
3 strands

Wrapped Backstitch
green
3 strands

Stem Stitch
turquoise 3 strands

Smyrna Stitch
yellow 3 strands

Satin Stitch
turquoise 3 strands

Satin Stitch
pink 3 strands

French Knot
dk brown 2 strands

Backstitch
blue 3 strands

Backstitch
brown 3 strands

Stem Stitch
blue 3 strands

Stem Stitch
blue 3 strands

Straight Stitch
brown 3 strands

Running Stitch
turquoise 3 strands

Lazy Daisy
turquoise 3 strands

Backstitch
blue 3 strands

embroidery floss:	DMC	Anchor
turquoise	964	185
blue	322	978
pink	899	52
yellow	3822	295
gold	972	298
brown	3826	1049
green	905	257
dk brown	3371	382

Top: Classical Elegance
Bottom: Fantasy Bloom

Fantasy Bloom

Materials
- ¼ yd of light green fabric
- ½ yd of burgundy brocade fabric
- 8 magenta plated beads, 3mm
- 280 dark green seed beads, 2mm
- 14-inch square pillow insert
- 2 yds burgundy cording

Instructions
1. Cut 15½ x 6-inch strip of lt green fabric. (If using embroidery hoop, cut strip large enough to fit.)
2. Transfer design on page 45 to fabric. *(See Transfer Techniques on page 6.)*
3. Embroider design referring to diagram and photograph for stitches and floss colors.
4. Cut two strips of burgundy fabric 15½ x 6 inches.
5. Sew strips of burgundy fabric to top and bottom of lt green fabric, right sides together, with ½-inch seams.

6. Press seams toward burgundy fabric.
7. Position cording ½ inch from edge of pillow front at the middle of the pillow front, leaving a 2-inch piece of cording free. Stitch close to cording with a zipper foot, overlapping a 2-inch end piece over the beginning piece.
8. Cut 15 x 15-inch square of burgundy fabric for backing.
9. With right sides together, stitch burgundy fabric to embroidered fabric around edges, leaving 8-inch opening to allow for turning.
10. Turn right side out, insert pillow and slipstitch opening closed.

Classical Elegance

Materials
- ½ yd tan fabric
- ½ yd backing fabric
- 18-inch square of cotton batting
- 16-inch square pillow insert
- 2 yds of off-white cording

Instructions
1. Cut 20-inch square from tan fabric.
2. Transfer designs on pages 46 and 47 to tan square. *(See Transfer Techniques on page 6.)*. You will need to join the two design patterns, then flip them over to complete the symmetrical pattern.
2. Embroider design referring to diagram and photograph for stitches and floss colors.
3. Position cording ½ inch from edge of pillow front, leaving a 2-inch piece of cording free. Stitch close to cording with a zipper foot, overlapping a

2-inch end piece over the beginning piece.
4. Pin batting to inside of embroidered fabric.
5. Cut 20-inch square from backing fabric. With right sides together, stitch backing fabric to embroidered fabric, leaving 9-inch opening to allow for turning.
6. Turn right side out, insert pillow and slipstitch opening closed.

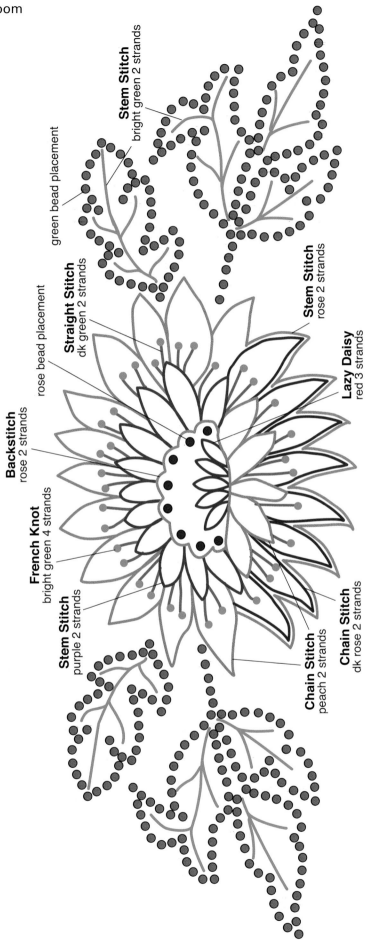

Stem Stitch
bright green 2 strands

green bead placement

Straight Stitch
dk green 2 strands

rose bead placement

Stem Stitch
rose 2 strands

Lazy Daisy
red 3 strands

Backstitch
rose 2 strands

French Knot
bright green 4 strands

Stem Stitch
purple 2 strands

Chain Stitch
peach 2 strands

Chain Stitch
dk rose 2 strands

embroidery floss:	DMC	Anchor
purple	327	100
dk rose	3803	69
rose	316	1017
red	3801	1098
peach	352	9
bright green	704	256
dk green	699	923

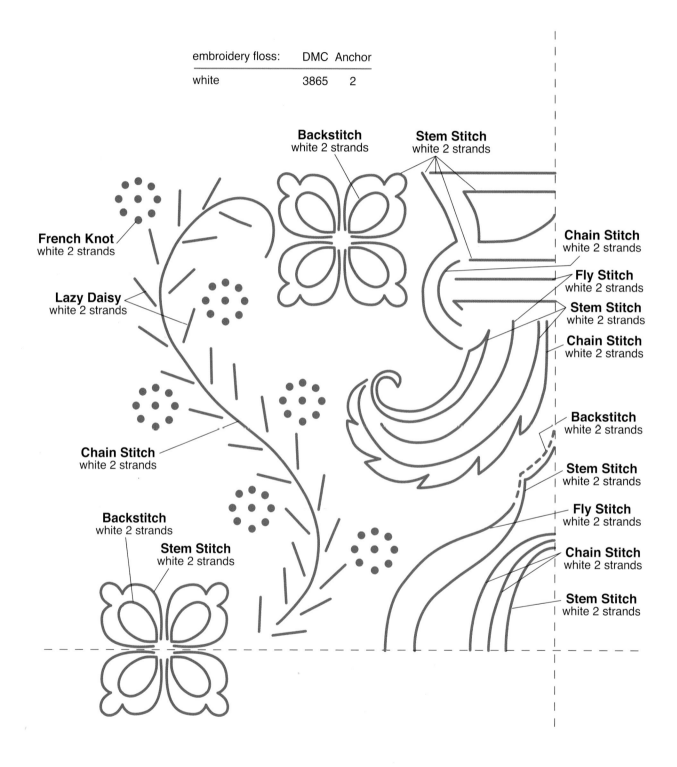

embroidery floss:	DMC	Anchor
white	3865	2

Backstitch
white 2 strands

Stem Stitch
white 2 strands

French Knot
white 2 strands

Lazy Daisy
white 2 strands

Chain Stitch
white 2 strands

Backstitch
white 2 strands

Stem Stitch
white 2 strands

Chain Stitch
white 2 strands

Fly Stitch
white 2 strands

Stem Stitch
white 2 strands

Chain Stitch
white 2 strands

Backstitch
white 2 strands

Stem Stitch
white 2 strands

Fly Stitch
white 2 strands

Chain Stitch
white 2 strands

Stem Stitch
white 2 strands

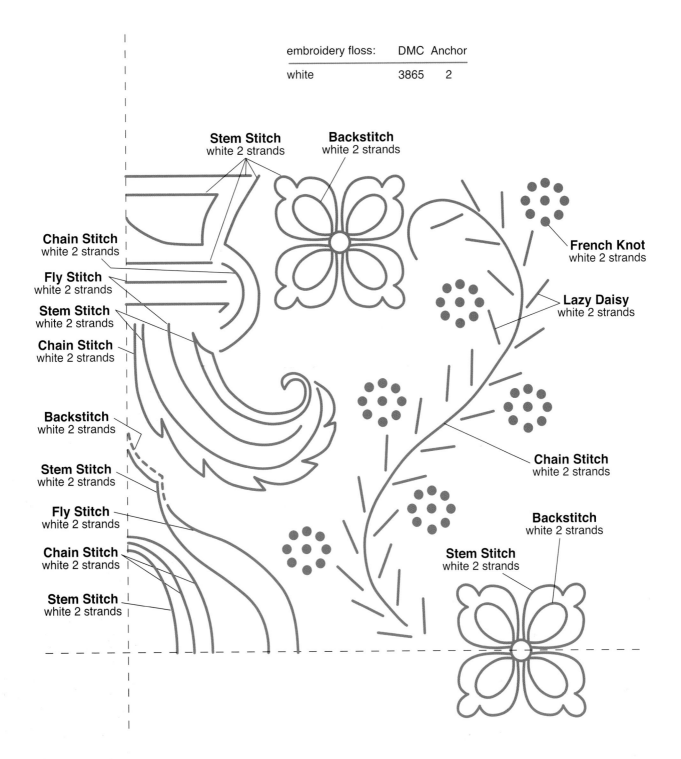

embroidery floss:	DMC	Anchor
white	3865	2

Stem Stitch
white 2 strands

Backstitch
white 2 strands

Chain Stitch
white 2 strands

Fly Stitch
white 2 strands

Stem Stitch
white 2 strands

Chain Stitch
white 2 strands

Backstitch
white 2 strands

Stem Stitch
white 2 strands

Fly Stitch
white 2 strands

Chain Stitch
white 2 strands

Stem Stitch
white 2 strands

French Knot
white 2 strands

Lazy Daisy
white 2 strands

Chain Stitch
white 2 strands

Backstitch
white 2 strands

Stem Stitch
white 2 strands

Hanging: Rock-a-Bye Baby Wall Hanging
Below: Day & Night Pillow

Day & Night Pillow

Materials
- ¼ yd lt blue cotton
- Scraps of lavender print and white/blue polka dot cotton fabrics
- ¼ yd lt blue and white print fabric
- ½ yd cotton backing fabric
- Polyester fiberfill

Instructions

1. Cut one 5-inch square from lt blue fabric. (If using embroidery hoop, cut square large enough to fit.)

2. Transfer sun design onto blue fabric. *(See Transfer Techniques on page 6.)*

3. Embroider design referring to diagram and photograph for stitches and floss colors.

4. Cut one 4-inch square from lt blue fabric. (If using embroidery hoop, cut square large enough to fit.)

5. Transfer moon design onto blue fabric. *(See Transfer Techniques on page 6.)*

6. Embroider design referring to diagram and photograph for stitches and floss colors.

7. Cut one 4 x 5-inch rectangle from polka dot fabric. Stitch to right side of sun square. Press seam toward blue fabric.

8. Cut one 5 x 4-inch rectangle from lavender fabric. Stitch to left side of moon square. Press seam toward blue fabric.

9. Stitch pieced sections together to form a square with sun on upper left side and moon on lower right side. Press seams to one side.

10. Cut four 3 x 13½-inch strips from blue and white print fabric. Starting and stopping ¼-inch from each edge, center and stitch the strips to the top, bottom and sides of the pieced square. Miter the corners. *(See Mitered Corners on page 63.)* Press.

11. Cut one 13½-inch square from backing fabric. With right sides together, stitch pillow front to backing fabric, leaving a 6-inch opening to allow for turning.

12. Trim excess fabric from corners. Turn right side out and press.

13. On pillow front, stitch through all layers ¾ inch from outside edge of pillow, leaving 6-inch opening.

14. Insert fiberfill. Slipstitch opening closed. Complete the stitching line on the top of the pillow.

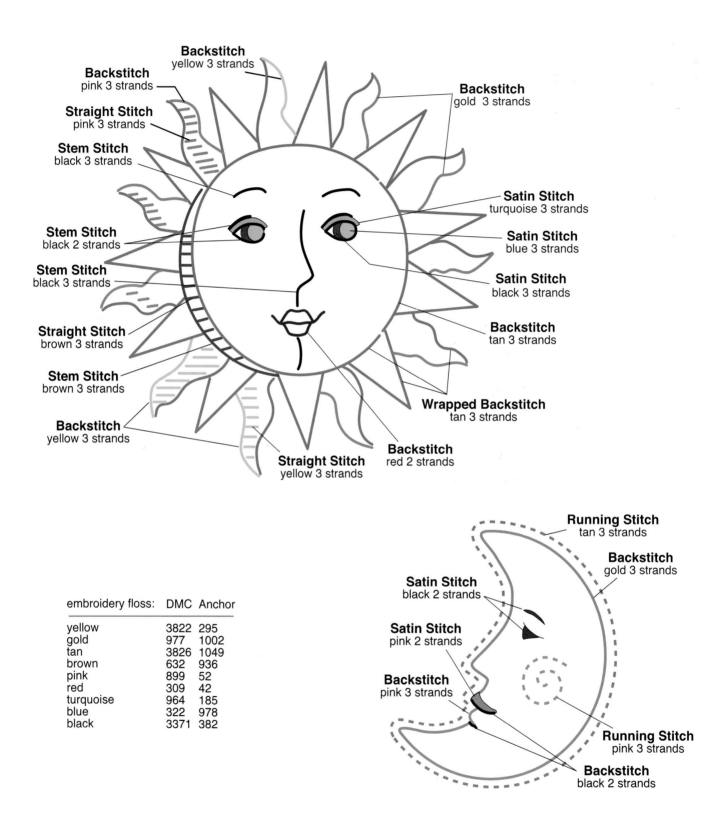

Backstitch
yellow 3 strands

Backstitch
pink 3 strands

Straight Stitch
pink 3 strands

Stem Stitch
black 3 strands

Stem Stitch
black 2 strands

Stem Stitch
black 3 strands

Straight Stitch
brown 3 strands

Stem Stitch
brown 3 strands

Backstitch
yellow 3 strands

Backstitch
yellow 3 strands

Backstitch
gold 3 strands

Satin Stitch
turquoise 3 strands

Satin Stitch
blue 3 strands

Satin Stitch
black 3 strands

Backstitch
tan 3 strands

Wrapped Backstitch
tan 3 strands

Straight Stitch
yellow 3 strands

Backstitch
red 2 strands

Running Stitch
tan 3 strands

Backstitch
gold 3 strands

Satin Stitch
black 2 strands

Satin Stitch
pink 2 strands

Backstitch
pink 3 strands

Running Stitch
pink 3 strands

Backstitch
black 2 strands

embroidery floss:	DMC	Anchor
yellow	3822	295
gold	977	1002
tan	3826	1049
brown	632	936
pink	899	52
red	309	42
turquoise	964	185
blue	322	978
black	3371	382

Rock-a-Bye Baby Wall Hanging

Materials
- ¼ yd white cotton fabric
- 1 yd lt blue print cotton fabric
- Scraps of lt turquoise, lt blue print, lavender print, and turquoise print cotton fabric
- 26-inch square of cotton batting
- 26-inch square cotton backing fabric
- Two ¼-inch buttons
- ½ yd fabric for binding

Instructions

1. Cut 7-inch square of white fabric. (If using embroidery hoop, cut square large enough to fit.)

2. Transfer baby design onto white square. *(See Transfer Techniques on page 6.)*

3. Embroider design referring to diagram and photograph for stitches and floss colors.

4. Cut four 3¾-inch squares from lt turquoise fabric. (If using embroidery hoop, cut squares large enough to fit.)

5. Transfer butterfly design to two lt turquoise squares and flower design to two lt turquoise squares.

6. Embroider designs referring to diagram and photograph for stitches and floss colors.

7. Cut eight 3¾-inch squares from the remaining scrap fabric.

8. Stitch two of these squares together then stitch to the top of the embroidered baby square **(Fig 1)**. Press seams to one side.

9. Stitch two more squares together; stitch to bottom of embroidered baby square **(Fig 1)**. Press seams to one side.

10. Stitch together one vertical strip with flower at top, two scrap squares, and butterfly at bottom. Stitch strip to left side of pieced rectangle **(Fig 2)**. Press seams toward vertical strip.

11. Stitch together one vertical strip with butterfly at top, two scrap squares, and flower at bottom. Stitch strip to right side of pieced rectangle **(Fig 2)**. Press seams toward vertical strip.

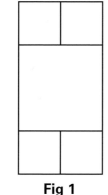

Fig 1

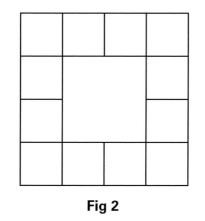

Fig 2

12. Cut four 6½ x 25½-inch strips from lt blue print fabric. Starting and stopping ¼ inch from each edge, center and stitch the strips to top, bottom and sides of wall hanging. Miter the corners **(Fig 3)**. *(See Mitered Corners on page 63.)* Press.

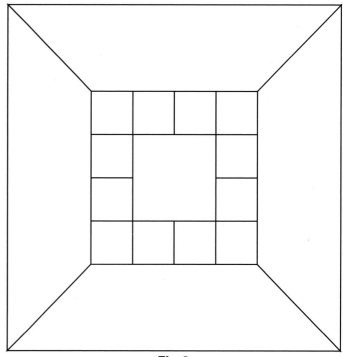

Fig 3

13. Place backing fabric, wrong side up, on work surface. Place batting on backing fabric. Place wall hanging, right side up, on batting. Pin or baste through all layers. Machine quilt as desired. *(See Machine Quilting on page 63)*

14. Trim edges even. Pin or baste edges.

15. Cut binding strips from fabric and attach to wall hanging. *(See Attaching the Binding on page 63.)*

16. Stitch buttons to bottom corners of embroidered baby square.

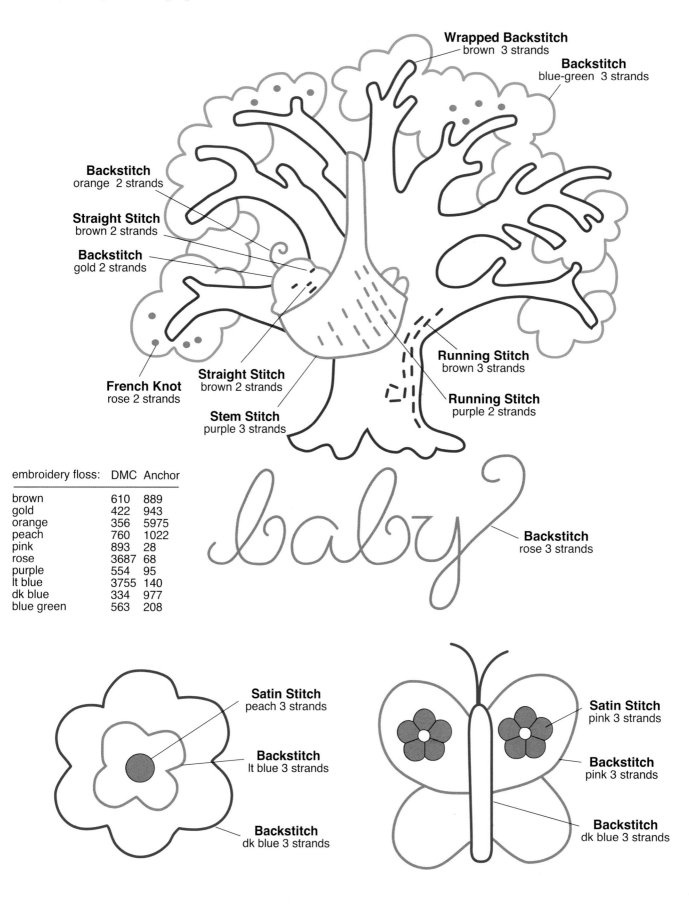

Wrapped Backstitch
brown 3 strands

Backstitch
blue-green 3 strands

Backstitch
orange 2 strands

Straight Stitch
brown 2 strands

Backstitch
gold 2 strands

French Knot
rose 2 strands

Straight Stitch
brown 2 strands

Stem Stitch
purple 3 strands

Running Stitch
brown 3 strands

Running Stitch
purple 2 strands

Backstitch
rose 3 strands

embroidery floss:	DMC	Anchor
brown	610	889
gold	422	943
orange	356	5975
peach	760	1022
pink	893	28
rose	3687	68
purple	554	95
lt blue	3755	140
dk blue	334	977
blue green	563	208

Satin Stitch
peach 3 strands

Backstitch
lt blue 3 strands

Backstitch
dk blue 3 strands

Satin Stitch
pink 3 strands

Backstitch
pink 3 strands

Backstitch
dk blue 3 strands

Baby's Bunny Wall Hanging

Baby's Bunny Wall Hanging

Materials
- ¾ yd white cotton fabric
- ¾ yd turquoise print cotton fabric
- ⅓ yd pink cotton fabric
- Scrap of orange cotton fabric
- Scrap of yellow print cotton fabric
- 26 x 25-inch piece of batting
- 26 x 25-inch piece of cotton backing fabric
- ⅜ yd fabric for binding
- 12 inches of turquoise silk ribbon, 7mm

Instructions

1. Cut three 4-inch squares from white fabric. (If using embroidery hoop, cut squares large enough to fit.)
2. Transfer cabbage and carrot design to each white square. *(See Transfer Techniques on page 6.)*
3. Embroider designs referring to diagram and photograph for stitches and floss colors.
4. Cut two 1¼ x 4-inch strips from yellow fabric. Stitch the strips between the cabbage and carrot squares to make a vertical row **(Fig 1)**. Press seams toward yellow fabric.
5. Cut one 2 x 12½-inch strip from white fabric. Stitch to left side of vertical cabbage and carrot row **(Fig 2)**. Press seam toward vertical strip.

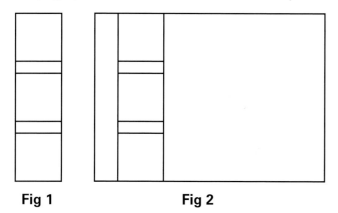

Fig 1   **Fig 2**

6. Cut one 14 x 12½-inch rectangle from white fabric. Stitch rectangle to right side of vertical cabbage and carrot row. Press seam toward large rectangle.
7. Cut scalloped border from 10¾ x 9¼-inch rectangle of pink fabric using pattern (page 57). Place on white rectangle, referring to photgraph for placement. Pin in place and zigzag stitch around outside and inside edges.
8. Cut three carrot designs from orange fabric and place on white rectangle, referring to photograph

for placement. Pin in place and zigzag stitch around edges.
9. Cut three 3-inch lengths from ribbon. Pin one length to the top of each carrot, so that half of the length extends from the top of the carrot. Refer to photograph for placement. Stitch through center of ribbon. Fold ribbon at angle forming a V and stitch through remaining ribbon section. Trim ends.
10. Transfer alphabet letters for desired name onto white rectangle, between carrots and top of pink border, using alphabet on page 56.
11. Embroider name in your choice of floss color, using backstitch, 2 strands.
12. Cut 19½ x 4½-inch strip from white fabric. (If using embroidery hoop, cut pieces large enough to fit.)
13. Embroider two repeats of rabbit/carrot design referring to diagram and photograph for stitches and floss colors.

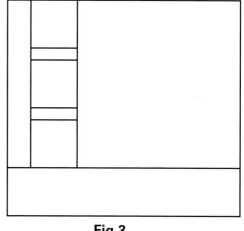

Fig 3

14. Stitch strip to bottom of the pieced rectangle **(Fig 3)**. Press seam toward rectangle.

15. Cut 3¾ x 19½-inch strip from turquoise fabric. Stitch to top of wall hanging **(Fig 4)**. Press seam toward turquoise fabric.

16. Cut two 3¾ x 19¾-inch strips from turquoise fabric. Stitch to sides of wall hanging **(Fig 4)**. Press.

17. Cut one 3¾ x 26¼-inch strip from turquoise fabric. Stitch to bottom of wall hanging **(Fig 4)**. Press.

18. Place backing fabric, wrong side up, on the work surface. Place batting on backing fabric. Place wall hanging top right side up on batting. Pin or baste through all layers. Machine quilt as desired.*(See Machine Quilting on page 63.)*

19. Cut binding strips from fabric and attach to wall hanging. *(See Attaching the Binding on page 63.)*

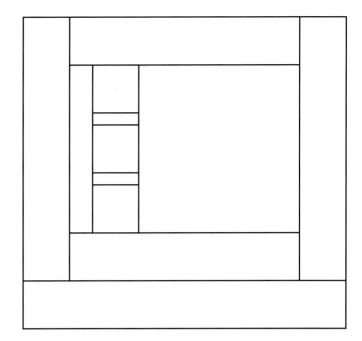

Fig 4

Backstitch
med green 3 strands

Backstitch
orange 3 strands

Straight Stitch
orange 3 strands

Running Stitch
pink 3 strands

Backstitch
dk brown 2 strands

French Knot
dk brown 2 strands

Backstitch
pink 3 strands

Backstitch
orange 3 strands

Backstitch
bright green
3 strands

Straight Stitch
orange 3 strands

Running Stitch
lt green 3 strands

Backstitch
lt green 3 strands

Straight Stitch
lt green 3 strands

embroidery floss:	DMC	Anchor
med green	563	208
lt green	564	206
bright green	704	256
orange	352	9
pink	3687	68
dk brown	3781	1050

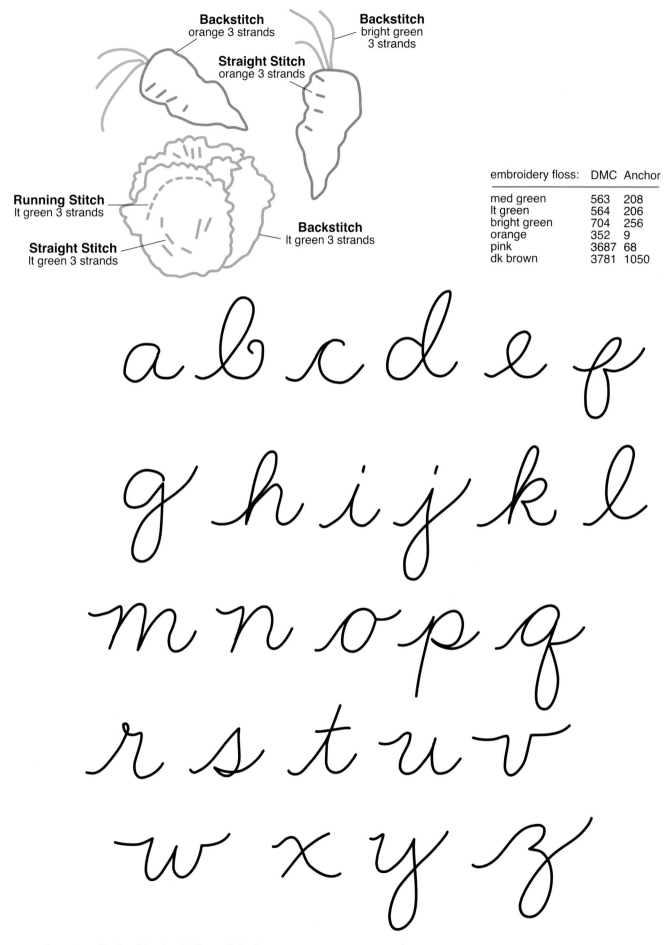

a b c d e f
g h i j k l
m n o p q
r s t u v
w x y z

Baby's Bunny Wall Hanging

Carrot Pattern
Full Size

Scallop Pattern
Full Size
Cut from 10¾ x 9¼-inch
rectangle of pink fabric

Friends Forever Wall Hanging

Friends Forever Wall Hanging

Materials
- ⅓ yd white cotton fabric
- ¾ yd green cotton fabric
- ½ yd blue paisley cotton fabric
- ¼ yd blue pin-dot cotton fabric
- 24 x 32-inch piece of batting
- 24 x 32-inch piece of cotton backing fabric
- ¼ yd fabric for binding

Instructions

1. Cut 8½ x 8-inch rectangle from white fabric. (If using embroidery hoop, cut rectangle large enough to fit.)
2. Transfer Friends design onto white rectangle. *(See Transfer Techniques on page 6.)*
3. Embroider design referring to diagram and photograph for stitches and floss colors.
4. Cut two 1¾ x 8½-inch strips from green fabric. Stitch strips to sides of embroidered rectangle **(Fig 1)**. Press.
5. Cut two 1¾ x 11-inch strips from green fabric. Stitch strips to top and bottom of embroidered rectangle **(Fig 1)**. Press.
6. Cut two 3½ x 11-inch strips from blue paisley fabric. Stitch to sides of pieced rectangle **(Fig 2)**. Press.
7. Cut two 3½ x 17½-inch strips from blue paisley fabric. Stitch to top and bottom of pieced rectangle **(Fig 2)**. Press.

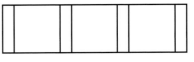

Fig 1

(If using embroidery hoop, cut squares large enough to fit.)
10. Transfer one basket design to each white square.
11. Embroider designs referring to diagram and photograph for stitches and floss colors.
12. Cut four 1¾ x 4½-inch strips from green fabric. Stitch basket pieces between strips to make horizontal row **(Fig 3)**. Press.

Fig 3

13. Stitch basket row to bottom of pieced rectangle **(Fig 4)**. Press.

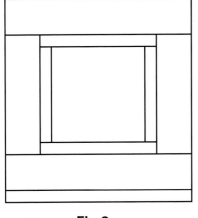

Fig 2

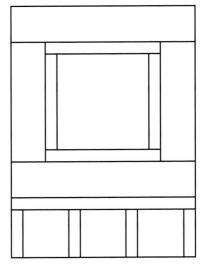

Fig 4

8. Cut one 2 x 17½-inch strip from blue pin dot fabric. Stitch to bottom of pieced rectangle **(Fig 2)**. Press.
9. Cut three 4½-inch squares from white fabric.

14. Cut one 4 x 17½-inch strip from blue pin-dot fabric. Stitch to bottom of pieced rectangle. Press.

15. Cut two 3¼ x 26-inch strips from green fabric. Stitch to sides of wall hanging **(Fig 5)**. Press.

16. Cut two 3¼ x 23-inch strips from green fabric. Stitch to top and bottom of wall hanging **(Fig 5)**. Press.

17. Place backing fabric wrong side up on work surface. Place batting on backing fabric. Place wall hanging, right side up, on batting. Pin or baste through all layers. Machine quilt as desired. *(See Machine Quilting on page 63.)*

18. Trim edges even. Pin or baste edges. Cut binding strips from fabric and attach to wall hanging. *(See Attaching the Binding on page 63.)*

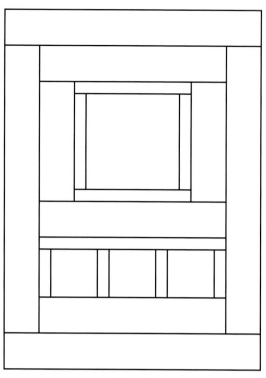

Fig 5

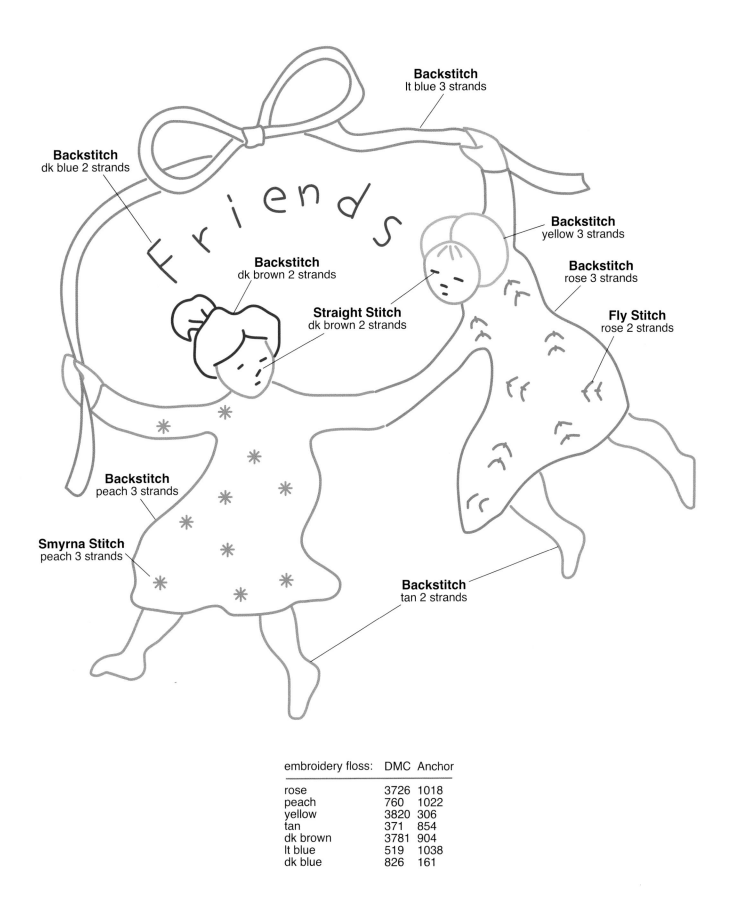

Backstitch
lt blue 3 strands

Backstitch
dk blue 2 strands

Backstitch
dk brown 2 strands

Backstitch
yellow 3 strands

Backstitch
rose 3 strands

Straight Stitch
dk brown 2 strands

Fly Stitch
rose 2 strands

Backstitch
peach 3 strands

Smyrna Stitch
peach 3 strands

Backstitch
tan 2 strands

embroidery floss:	DMC	Anchor
rose	3726	1018
peach	760	1022
yellow	3820	306
tan	371	854
dk brown	3781	904
lt blue	519	1038
dk blue	826	161

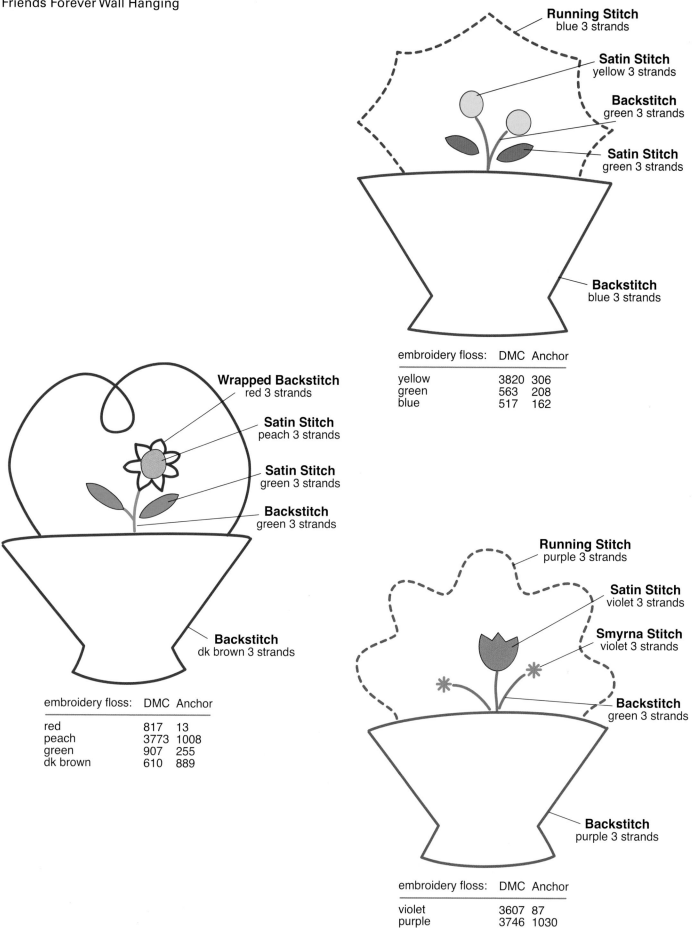

Running Stitch
blue 3 strands

Satin Stitch
yellow 3 strands

Backstitch
green 3 strands

Satin Stitch
green 3 strands

Backstitch
blue 3 strands

embroidery floss:	DMC	Anchor
yellow	3820	306
green	563	208
blue	517	162

Wrapped Backstitch
red 3 strands

Satin Stitch
peach 3 strands

Satin Stitch
green 3 strands

Backstitch
green 3 strands

Backstitch
dk brown 3 strands

embroidery floss:	DMC	Anchor
red	817	13
peach	3773	1008
green	907	255
dk brown	610	889

Running Stitch
purple 3 strands

Satin Stitch
violet 3 strands

Smyrna Stitch
violet 3 strands

Backstitch
green 3 strands

Backstitch
purple 3 strands

embroidery floss:	DMC	Anchor
violet	3607	87
purple	3746	1030
dk green	3345	268

Make all squares and rectangles as specified with the individual project instructions. Sew the pieces together referring to the wall hanging layouts and step-by-step instructions.

Layering

There are many types of batting on the market. For wall hangings, choose a thin cotton or polyester batting. Use 100% cotton fabric for the backing of the wall hanging. Cut backing and batting about 2 inches larger on all sides than the top of the wall hanging. Place backing wrong side up, then smooth out batting on top. Center top right side up on batting. Baste layers together.

Machine Quilting

You do not need a special machine to quilt your wall hanging. Just make sure your machine is oiled and in good working condition. An even-feed foot is a good investment if you are going to machine quilt, since it is designed to feed the top and bottom layers of the wall hanging through the machine evenly.

To quilt in-the-ditch of a seam (this is stitching in the space between two pieces of fabric that have been sewn together), use your fingers to pull blocks or pieces apart slightly and machine stitch right between the two pieces. Try to keep stitching to the side of the seam that does not have the bulk of the seam allowance under it. When you have finished stitching, the quilting will be practically hidden in the seam.

Attaching the Binding

Trim backing and batting even with wall hanging top. For side edges, measure the wall hanging top lengthwise; cut two 2-inch wide strips that length. Fold strips in half lengthwise, wrong sides

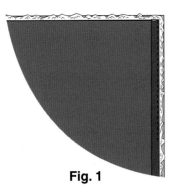

Fig. 1

together. Place one strip along one side of the wall hanging; sew with a ¼-inch seam allowance. **(Fig 1)**

Turn binding to back and slipstitch to backing, covering previous stitching line. **(Fig 2)** Repeat on other side.

Fig. 2

For top and bottom edges, measure wall hanging crosswise and cut two 2-inch strips that length, adding ½- inch to each end. Fold strips in half lengthwise with wrong sides together. Place one strip along top edge with ½ inch extending beyond each side; sew with a ¼-inch seam allowance. **(Fig 3)**

Fig. 3

Turn binding to back and tuck the extra ½ inch under at each end; slipstitch to backing fabric. Repeat at bottom edge.

Mitered Corners

To miter corners, fold wall hanging in half diagonally; border ends will be right sides together, extending past wall hanging. Draw diagonal line on border even with diagonal fold of wall hanging. Sew along drawn line. Check miter to see if it is even, then trim corner from seam. Repeat at remaining corners.

Our thanks to Fairfield Processing Corp. for providing materials used in this book.

DRG Publishing
306 East Parr Road
Berne, IN 46711

©2004 American School of Needlework
TOLL-FREE ORDER LINE or to request a free catalog (800)582-6643
Customer Service (800) 282-6643, **Fax** (800)882-6643

Visit www.AnniesAttic.com